D1584341

JAMIE MCKENDRICK

Out There

_____

faber and faber

First published in 2012
by Faber and Faber Ltd
Bloomsbury House
74–77 Great Russell Street
London WC1B 3DA

Typeset by CB editions, London
Printed in England by T. J. International Ltd, Padstow, Cornwall

The right of Jamie McKendrick to be identified as author
of this work has been asserted in accordance with Section 77
of the Copyright, Designs and Patents Act 1988

A CIP record for this book
is available from the British Library

ISBN 978-0-571-28911-0

FSC
www.fsc.org
MIX
Paper from
responsible sources
FSC® C101712

2 4 6 8 10 9 7 5 3 1

Questo aiuolo che ci fa tanto feroci
(This little patch of earth that makes us all so fierce)

Dante, *Paradiso*

Acknowledgements and Notes

I am grateful to the editors of the following publications where these poems first appeared: *Financial Times*, *Granta* (100 and 119), *London Review of Books*, *Modern Poetry in Translation*, *New Statesman*, *Poetry London*, *Poetry Review*, *Qualm*, *Spectator*, *The Stinging Fly*, *Times Literary Supplement*, *World Literature Today*; and to the editors of these anthologies: *Best British Poetry 2012* (ed. Sasha Dugdale, Salt), *Dark Matter* (ed. Maurice Riordan and Joyce Bell Burnell, Calouste Gulbenkian,), *The Laurel Crown* (ed. Jemimah Kuhfeld), *The Living Planet* (ed. Mary Green, Cambridge University Press), *London: A History in Verse* (ed. Mark Ford, Harvard University Press), *Poems on the Underground: A New Edition* (ed. Gerard Benson, Judith Chernaik and Cicely Herbert, Penguin) *See How I Land: Oxford Poets and Exiled Writers* (ed. Carole Angier, Rachel Buxton, Stephanie Kitchen and Simon White, Heaventree Press).

'Outcasts' was commissioned by Hear! Here! (BBC and Royal Philharmonic) and published on their website.
'Entropy in Wiesbaden', translated from the Mexican poet David Huerta, was originally commissioned by Sarah Maguire at The Translation Workshop and published in a chapbook *David Huerta: Poemas/Poems*, edited by Tom Boll.

I'm indebted to the scientist and writer Dr Kevin Fong for his vivid account of the physical and mental effects of space travel to which I refer in 'Out There'.

The events retold in 'Odyssey' were related to me by Ebi Karimi and I'm most grateful to him for his permission to republish it.

'The Seventh Planet' and 'The Deadhouse' were commissioned by Romesh Gunesekera and Somerset House for the sound installation 'River Sounding' by Bill Fontana. The Deadhouse itself is situated in the basement of Somerset House and contains several gravestones set in the wall. The lines in French are taken from one of the inscriptions.

Details in the poem 'The Lepers' Plot (1321)' are drawn from Carlo Ginzburg's *Ecstacies: Deciphering the Witches' Sabbath* (translation by Raymond Rosenthal).

Contents

OUT THERE

Out There

If space begins at an indefinite zone
where the chance of two gas molecules colliding
is rarer than a green dog or a blue moon
then that's as near as we can get to nothing.

Nostalgia for the earth and its atmosphere
weakens the flesh and bones of cosmonauts.
One woke to find his crewmate in a space suit
and asked where he was going. For a walk.

He had to sleep between him and the air-lock.
Another heard a dog bark and a child cry
halfway to the moon. What once had been

where heaven was, is barren beyond imagining,
and never so keenly as from out there can
the lost feel earth's the only paradise.

On Nothing

I do not think it is absurd for you to say that nothing is something,
since no one can deny that 'nothing' is a noun.
Anselm of Canterbury

If nothing is the opposite of something
then it too is something and not nothing.
Or is that just language rushing in
to fill what makes the intellect recoil?

It's us not nature that abhors a vacuum,
for in frictionless space there's still a fraction
more than nothing, if not enough of it
to slow the planets in their orbits.

But the full moon hides its emptiness
and every plenitude its opposite;
the present buckles into nowlessness

that lasts for never as a dark star draws
downward threads of light. There nothing exists,
couching like a sphinx among the rubble.

The Perils

*Think of the perils of seafarers and the perils of travellers by
land! Anyone walking anywhere is liable to sudden accidents . . .
One would suppose the sitting posture to be perfectly safe.
And yet . . .*
St Augustine, *The City of God*

We may be wise enough to shun the waves
but only folly would suppose
the land is safe: land is deeper than the sea.
Rock, sand and soil all have their perils.

Quakes raze and floods submerge our habitations.
One bite from a rabid dog makes man feared
by his own family as much as any
wild beast. The body itself is heir to

more foul diseases than the books
of physicians can accommodate.
Walking anywhere is constant danger.

Even seated at my desk to write this
I remember the priest Eli who fell
from his chair never to rise again.

The Seventh Planet

*discovered by William Herschel with a reflector
telescope, 13/3/1781*

For the inhabitants of or an observer on
Uranus, whose poles are its equator,
our polar weather would be an unimaginable dog day.

The force of its grizzled winds does not permit
the elevation of any permanent structures
except those afforded by tempered ice or rooted rock

and mostly the depth of methane cloud makes day
indistinguishable from deepest starless night.
But having so many moons which all exert

divergent tugs on the giant planet's frozen tides
makes each being a whole continent of moods.
Their hearts signal colours brighter than a cuttlefish

beneath a glacier shield, though it's easy enough
to keep your distance till the summer equinox
when acid rain falls vertical not slantwise

and speech returns, the engine of an avalanche,
either tormented lyric or exuberant lament.

A Safe Distance

If the moon were closer, quite apart
from disasters it would wreak on earth,
how soon before that chiaroscuro,
the light-splashed pores and shadowy pits,
engrossing so much of the night sky
and dimming half the constellations,
would start to pall? By the same rule
the distance that divides us seems
providentially assigned so that
from here you still look radiant, majestic.

From the Flood Plain

No flood as parched as this – a mere foot
or two of gilded bilge – will turf us out
from the lands of the frog and the newt
who for the best part of a century
have bided our time in the tall grass.
We've stood their ground, and stand it still,
though our legs are cased in long green boots
and the sofa's propped on a tower of bricks.

Unmoved, we see fish swim in the back yard
and a swan sneer from the vicar's garden,
though the cold waters still keep rising,
working away at the silicone seals,
unpicking the doors we've turned into dykes
and days may pass before our power's restored.

Après

When the flood waters left they left
the pine boards cupped; the plaster blistered
with salts; the cheap chipboard
bursting out of its laminate jacket
in all the kitchen units; the electrics wrecked
with the wires firing in the sockets;
the polyfilled cracks in the buckled doors
once more agape; the iron grate sporting
a hem of rust and the ash it contained
arranged in a scum-line above the skirting;
dampness, months-deep, fattening the pores
of the brickwork; a question mark over the slate floor;
the oven fouled; the fridge unsafe; the whole place
humming with marsh rot and fetor
but the garden, the garden good, and greener
for an alien crop of hogweed higher
than us, hardy, sturdy, hirsute, armed
with a poison sap against expulsion.

Teazles

Out in the vacant lot to gather weeds
I found these teazles – their ovoid heads
delicately armoured with crowns of thorns.
Arthur, from whom I haven't heard a word
in thirty years, who must be ninety if
he's a day, told me they were used to raise
the nap on the green felt of billiards tables
and, since Roman times, for combing woollen stuff.
He also said their seeds were caviar
to the goldfinch. And then I lost the knife
he'd lent me to cut some – the loss of which
was the cause of grief. In honour of gruff Arthur
I shake the seeds out in our small green patch
and stick the spiky seed heads in a jar.

Bark

A tour of all the trees that grow
in Barcelona's port was my reward
for buzzing, uninvited, at María's door.
She knew each one by name and character:
oleander, tamarind, the four or five
orders of palm, Corinthian-topped or
plain Ionic. But the *palo borracho*
was unlike anything I'd seen before:
its every inch of bark a skewering spike
worse than a bite: horrid, arid, hard
as nails, leaving nothing unprotected
but a few pink flowers. Ogre-like, unlike
us, who harden grimmer year by year,
with age it sheds the armour that it wore.

Oak

When my father saw an advert in the *Echo*
for a big house at a peppercorn rent
he rang and heard a voice with a slight croak
enquire – Can you read a map? – Yes. – OK
meet me tomorrow noon . . . (the voice gave co-ordinates).
So he drove through the green deep past Wenlock
and stopped in a lane beside a field gate
where soon another car appeared
and unburdened itself of an elderly gent.
– The name's Forester. (Eliding the Lord.)
He walked my father to the gate and asked
what he could see: at first, nothing but trees
in the distance. – D'you mean *that* . . . magnificent oak?
– The house is yours. I'll have them send the keys.

The Owls

Baudelaire, 'Les Hiboux'

Under the yew's black roof the owls,
more hewn than grown, sit like a shelf of gods
all in a row, while their fierce red eyes
measure what moves. They meditate

and keep that spectral attitude until
their own hour comes when the sun's rays fall
so low that shadow folds on shadow,
close as the sable feathers on their wings.

Let the wise learn from them there's nothing
so wasteful as human turmoil,
as changing places, changing skies – for all

you'll reap as your reward is
to find yourself forever climbing
the stairway to nowhere of a treadmill.

Door

Bartolo Cattafi, 'Porta'

Bare and humble offspring
of a common plant
squared off as God willed
resist them
with every fibre
brace yourself lengthways sideways
daub yourself with a sign of flaming paint
they will come by night
they'll hurl themselves upon you
in an avalanche
howling with outspread wings
with punches kicks and curses
with the heads of rams
the stink of sulphur.

The Gate

Door – *1. The gate of a house; that which opens to yield entrance.*
Door *is used of houses, and* gates *of cities or publick buildings;*
except in the licence of poetry.
Samuel Johnson, *Dictionary of the English Language*

This sawn-off backdoor has become a gate,
nicely fitting a gap in the fence.
Unlike the door it was, the gate keeps
nothing out: not the creatures of jet and agate
nor the toads and newts that shuffle under
its ragged footrail. Least of all the flood that overflows
the reservoir and breaches all defences.
The gate unites the space it splits asunder
and lets you in to/out of, more or less
the same thing, joining green to green, earth

to earth: same light, same weather either side.
A superfluous barrier: openness
traverses it. Unbounded air ignores
the interruption. More art than function,
even if my neighbour, pointing at the paint
I half scraped off, just sees an eyesore.
As yet it yields to the slightest pressure,
but in time it may define a frontier, once more
divide the outside from the inside.
The door again, but of a redimensioned house.

The Literalist

When told they'd be made into fishers of men
did it not occur to a single one
that he'd be best off staying a fisher of fish,

reluctant to catch men with the lure of heaven
 – an electric-blue dragonfly threaded
on an iron hook? That he'd no heart to land

shoals of men ashore to breathe the wrong air,
or have them kneel before a statue's crimson tears
operated by a small pump in the vestry?

That he wanted fish to be fish, and not multiplied
ad infinitum by unearthliness;
wanted loaves to be loaves, salt waves to be waves

and not a secret floor the saviour walks on?
Just to sink when he sank and swim when he swam.

The Warning

I'd not seen the red flag posted on the beach
frantic in the *tramontana*, only the same waves
as the day before, big but not forbidding,

though it was odd in August there should be
no swimmers, only way out the indomitable
surfers sleek and in their element as porpoises.

So without a pause I went in and swam out
no more than twenty metres, then I turned
to see not hear you shouting from the shore

and, swimming back, it dawned on me each stroke
you seemed a fraction smaller. A figurine.
I cursed the air that suddenly was water,

the strength that had bled from my arms and legs
as the waves pummelled me like a gull's feather,
the current stronger than the will to live.

First and Last

Effect preceded cause: the storm
conjured the butterfly's wing, a dusky,

spattered wing, with a black quoit
afloat on a red ground; and the blasted oak

called forth the skittish thunderbolt;
and the earthquake that shook a city off

the earth's back had already tampered with
the continental plates; and the tremor I felt

when your face appeared made your face appear
a flawless catastrophe, prime mover and last word.

I fell but the fall preceded that first sight.

Rain

Borges, 'La Lluvia'

All at once the afternoon has cleared
as a fine specific rain begins to fall.
It falls, or fell. For as a rule the rain
happens in the past: it feels like rainfell.

Whoever hears it fall will find restored
the time when a marvellous stroke of luck
disclosed to him a flower named rose
and the odd colour of the word coloured.

This rain which blinds the window panes
brings joy in the lost suburbs to the black
grapes of a vine that grows

on a patio no longer there. The rain-haunted
afternoon brings me the voice, the longed-for voice
of my father coming home, no longer dead.

The Carved Buddha

Within the lotus bud of sandalwood that needs
to be pried open by a thumbnail the Buddha sits
cross-legged on a flower exuding the odour of resin
under a light coating of gold leaf.

It belonged to Mrs Ogilvie from Aberdeen:
when she opened the perfect fit of the upper lid
I knew that nothing made by the hand of man
could hold a candle to it. Its beauty blazed

but quietly, a tiny inexhaustible thing.
I instantly forgot the ban on brazen
idols, and remembered the mustard seed.

You could not guess what the small plain
capsule concealed, and when you saw
you guessed another light burnt from within.

The Meeting House

We have come to listen to the silence,
but the silence listens back at us.
Sparks in the blaze of its galactic dark,
we sit in a square that should have been a circle,

facing the oak table's bowl of oak leaves,
the Holy Bible overgrown with bark.
From the east window a sunbeam angles
down a ladder for the mute choir

of dust motes, or mites, or dancing atoms,
but no one breaks the silence which is made
from the base upwards like a bowl of clay,
as moments lapse into millennia

and minutes round into an hour. Then one
of the carved elders comes alive and shakes
his neighbour's hand: the room erupts in wood notes
as though a ladder's rungs were being strummed.

Psychostasia

On our way back from Hell (the mosaic)
well not just hell but the whole
escatos panoramically depicted
on the church wall of Torcello
we came across two reptiles
in mortal combat on a footbridge.

Sort of bantamweight as lizards go,
they looked grotesquely scaled-up, dinosauric,
ilk of the hissing Brazilian tortoises
in Albert Eckhout's masterpiece.
Same look of human fury on their faces,
though our own is obviously heroic.

The one that had its jaws clamped round the other's neck
let go as we approached but then the other

lunged at its tail: they writhed again in a green tangle
and the same death grip was re-established.

Their fate hung in the balance
of the gods, like Hector and Achilles,
– a bronze star bearing down in vengeful rage –
or like the souls being judged on the church wall
by the Archangel Michael
while the devils try to tip the scales

But for a counterweight to the human heart
– its truth so light – the ostrich feather's best
with the jackal Anubis holding the scales
and hippo-haunched, croc-snouted Ammut
couched among the papyrus, inert
and waiting to devour us.

The Judgement

The mosaic on the façade
of Prague's St Vitus cathedral
shows the damned all dressed up
as for some dance
but being dragged towards the mouth of hell
by demons with hooks and halberds
while the blessed are naked
gently lifted by angels
out of their gaping sepulchres
– you look twice kind of
expecting it to be the other way round
but it's not some Bohemian
naturist's whim rather
that the damned are attached to their
trappings their habits of concealment
& the blessed have nothing
to hide or be ashamed of

The nakedness of prisoners
before the smirking guards
taking cellphone snapshots
and with hellhounds
wrenching at the leash
is innocent however
guiltily they're massed
in a catasta of flesh

The Lepers' Plot (1321)

Snow for a month and death in the villages.
The sun turned blood red and the moon mildewed.
We rounded up the lepers and impounded
their goods, and branded them on the neck
with red-hot irons. More snow at Lent
and a great rain fell, flooding the fields.
The trials were held inside the monastery.
One confessed in agony that the Jews
had taught the lepers how to poison wells
with blood, urine, three herbs and the host,
all mixed and dried and sewn into a small sack
with a pebble to make it sink. Another told
how the King of Granada and the Sultan of Babylon
had planned to overthrow the whole of Christendom:
it was they who paid the Jews who then employed
the lepers, with the Devil's help always at hand,
to make the potion that brought about the plague.

If all were equal, the Jews told the lepers,
no one would despise their fellows. But see how
they treat you now with your scarlet hoods and rattles.
And we Jews must wear a yellow disc sewn to our clothes.
We must all become equal in sickness,
they said. Some Jews denied this truth
under torture, and died denying it, hardened
against the light to their last breath. We prayed
after the Jews and lepers had been burnt
that our brethren should be free from all infection.

Odyssey

'Burly, unscareable – only the rats
were at home in the camp at Patra
– you can see for yourself this foyer of hell
if you go on holiday to Greece.
I stayed, unsure how to leave, nine months in all,
apart from the two days in hospital
after being picked up by the police.
I survived, unlike Ali
whom I'd been with from the start – we'd argued
and agreed every step of the way, walking by
night through the mountains to Turkey,
avoiding landmines, praying for rain
to drink, rationing out the tinned food
we'd thought to bring, our trainers in tatters.

That day we had a lunch of rice
then said goodbye. He chose a lorry
he was hoping would board the ferry
to Ancona. You have to hold on for
dear life above the back axle
to a sheaf of oily wires – one pot-hole,
a sudden stop or an acceleration,
and chances are you'll lose your grip and fall.
To send his body back to Iran
would have cost many times more than
the few dollars we kept hidden
in a bar of soap, carefully hollowed out
and sculpted over. All we could do
was bury him by the camp at Patra.'

Cofiwch Dryweryn

Remember Tryweryn – graffiti near Aberystwyth

Soft water from Tryweryn reservoir
was at our fingertips
in Liverpool; no limescale clogged the taps
but imperceptible rogue molecules
ran from the drowned valley, the slate roofs and stone walls
of Capel Celyn, whose fifty souls
were cleared, while those in the Quaker graveyard
were gravelled over. Soft water from Wales
was all we knew, the shadow
of the 'giver' faded from the cup,
the singing flow like a foreign tongue
silenced by a twist. Billions of liquid tons
lie on their homes – soft, oblivious sips
which cushioned us from others' hardships.

Epithets

Toledo la rica, Salamanca la fuerte, Leon la bella,
Oviedo la sacra, y Sevilla la grande.

Liverpool the impoverished, the liverish, the void, the full,
the self-besotted, the blarney-argoted, the blitzed and
    blackened,
the *bella-brutta*, the rag-rich, the moss-stained sandstoned,
the green-lung'd, the ricket-ridden, the loud and adenoidal.

Liverpool the last-to-be-served, the least-accounted,
the over-arched and undermined, the mother-tongued and
    plurilingual,
the Catholic-Protestant, the cap-in-hand, the hand-
to-mouth, the pub-encrusted and the hovel-haunted.

Liverpool the riverine, the ocean-avid, the slaveship-tainted,
sugar-whitening, matchstick-making, slum and dockland
refuge of Lascars, Chinese, Irish, Jews, Somalians.

Liverpool the deserted, the polluted, the *de bon aire*,
the clinker-built and shipwrecked, the chameleon,
the edge-of-everywhere-and-nowhere's-centre.

El Puente de los Peligros, Murcia

for Mick Imlah

By the Bridge of Perils we looked down on the Segura,
'one of the most polluted rivers in Europe',
though safe enough for a colony of tortoises,
arrived from Africa, to be basking on a mud bank.

The day's task: to translate 'La Luna' by Borges,
and we were skiving off. I quoted mine
called 'Mooning' which shed a whole new light
on the final line: *¡Mírala! Es tu espejo.*

It won a smile. You were handsome as a Roman tortoise
as Lorca said of the Gaditan singer Ignacio Espeleta,
and no more than him inclined to work – within a day, the
    pretty
festival assistants had set their hearts on you.

But all the same, against the grain, you did work,
you did the work which overtook the hares
at the last curve – you couldn't have left it later
for *The Lost Leader* to nonchalantly lead the field.

Of course it's not a race or competition, and sport
always seemed to me the opposite of poems but for you
it's like they had a common source in speed, panache,
the human stripped of all accoutrements and props

facing its limits. I miss – word that does what it says –
those *cervezas* under the cathedral's
clashing Gothic and Baroque. I miss your swarthy Caledonian
duende, the deadpan pranks, the glinting wit,

your judgement's slow sure coil and lightning-quick release.

Ethics & Aesthetics

When Franco had Aranguren
the Professor of Ethics
in Madrid
fired
for his involvement in student politics

Barcelona's Professor of Aesthetics
the poet Valverde
resigned with a note that read
nulla aesthetica sine ethica

– gesture and word so wed
they twisted an *Either/Or*
into a well-knotted
ampersand

and fastened a rope bridge across a chasm

Injury

The injured man stares at the ground which did not open.
The words we find are not the right words

to take us back before this wrong completion,
before the wrong appeared which, then, might still have been

averted. We still believe things done might be undone,
the outcome other, but the words are fended off.

The injured man has only this defence, but none
against himself. He's joined the side of those against him.

He's joined the jury and the prosecution
and will not have a word said in his favour.

Only the ground, for now, seems on his side.
It did not open and it would not take him.

Toscanelli

Not knowing a soul in the frozen city, my ears
still pierced by the drum roll and trumpet blast
in the midnight square – hearse or rehearsal for
some summer pageant? – I lit the last
of the Tuscan cigars I'd bought in the hope
their vile taste of creosote that gave
Clint his grimace in the spaghetti westerns
might help me quit. But the acrid smoke
was company and conjured up instead
the packet of Toscanelli with the *tricolore*
that Ungaretti brought from Italy
to the top floor on Boulevard St Germain
where Apollinaire lay on his death bed
– but dropped them in shock when he saw the black
bandage round his friend's head, the trepanned head
from which had flowed so thick and fast
the words that orchestrated liberty.

The Deadhouse

Somerset House

Ooliths in a Jurassic bath of micrite:
the palatial, weathered white of Portland stone.
I too would prefer to watch the work of masons

than hear sermons. Watch them mallet down
the granite paving cubes, dress limestone,
engrave the slab of the Queen's Lady-in-Waiting:

CY GIST LE CORPS DE DEFVNCTE CATHERINE
GVILERMET. PRIEZ DIEV POVR SON AME.

*

Catchpool of sound in the sheer lightwell.
Catchpool of light in the deep soundwell.
A faint swell of water at the palace roots.

Ting-tang, the quarter chimes from the birdcage
cast frame in the West Wing, clock work
by Vulliamy. Its silent fellow in the East.

The rivergate now a sweeping arch left on
the stone manuscript. Bricked in, the river embanked.

*

Creases of thick water, iron-filed and polished.
Silken rucks as the river eases and edges past
the bridge, glistened, scuffed and scored like a zinc plate

half-cleared of ink. Fiddleheads of swirls,
fishtail eddies. Its own level. Sea level.
Rolled up seacharts like telescopes

in the Navy Board storeroom.
The thrumming engine of empire.

*

Mind-forged, unreal city. The weight
of stone on each square foot of earth.
At least the river is its own weight, give or take

the passing traffic. Makes a silvery tear
where the light floods in, pools in the soundwell.
Scaresome the outreach of its administrations,

the intent skulking in its bridges' shadows, its
tentacular, inky dusk with fishlamps scowling.

*

Loath to be lured to the glove of the falconer
with a strip of bush-meat the Harris hawk,
employed to chase pigeons from the Deadhouse,

perches on a lagged pipe, settles its gold tail-feathers
and glares at the tombstone of the king's priest.
Upstairs the taxes rendered unto Caesar

his own minted image or hologram,
while the river, withdrawn to a new margin,
reflects gold glass from the wavering,

hollow towers of commerce where the profiteers
long for their 'strong and stable government'.
The skaters wait till winter for their rink.

Last Visit

for Tom Lubbock

I was visiting you in your last days
as in life I'd failed to. Your speech was restored
though your movements were impaired.
You explained how the 'epidural'
climbed rib by rib up your vertebrae
but though of course the creeping
paralysis was horrible, the sensory
impressions it unleashed might be described
as beautiful. It must have been a memory
of my last visit when with a walking stick
you pointed to the Matisse postcard you could still
understand, but the Lautrec not, how
the CD of Monteverdi was too complicated
but Couperin was perfect, clear as day,
and then pointing, there and there, at what
I couldn't tell, though as in one of your pieces
that start so simply with a precise detail
then steadily move towards the depths, you seemed
to be fathoming things, in the room around,
which you hadn't seen before, mysterious
bright configurations and conjunctions
imperceptible to me as I followed
those brusque and almost joyous gesturings.

Mademoiselle Garde

His idea of a first date was a wrestling match
but it was him who left doubled up with stomach cramps
so I had to nurse him through the night – hence my name

Gerda became Garde. As in *Tu dois
être mon garde toujours* . . . closer than that
he never got to a proposal.

When Barnes, the Philadelphian millionaire,
bought fifty of his paintings he left
that talent factory & phalanstery La Ruche,

more ant heap than beehive, more haven than either,
and could suddenly buy whatever he pleased.
He bought a collection of identical silk hats

he never wore but hid his francs in
with a nervous disbelief that they were his.

*

He'd tell me off for speaking German, proud
as a dauphin of his fluent French. Don't you ever,
I asked in tears, don't you ever feel homesick?

A veiled look came into his eyes,
then for the first time he wrote a letter home
to Smilovichi, a shtetl near Minsk.

For months he waited, pent, but no reply.

*

He hunted down his old canvases
in the Quai d'Orléans and those he found
he'd shred with a razor in a fit of joy.

Bright strips: wind-flailed trees and Céret skies,
all felled, lay littering the floor. I longed to
sew those ruined worlds together, and restore him.

Him and the beauty he'd gone blind to.

*

Once he could barely afford food and now
he painted the meat and fish he couldn't eat
because of the pain. For hours in the country

he'd seek out four-leaved clovers like a child.
I'd say he was lucky but his luck arrived
too late to be of use. Though his passport read

Chaim Soutine. Connu comme juif
the police left him alone whereas I
was interned in a camp barracks in Gurs

with fifty Spanish women. Despite his promises,
months I heard nothing from him then
a package came with money and forged papers.

*

I returned to Paris and found him living
with Marie-Berthe Aurenche, Max Ernst's ex-wife
– what made her leave *his* Loplop Paradise?

He wouldn't see me so as not to hurt
her feelings. One day early August '43
the doorbell rang – I was sure it was the Gestapo,

but it was a telegram from her, telling me to call.
Which I knew could only mean one thing.
I heard her formal voice explaining

about the operation. The perforated ulcer
left too long. – I don't know if he was more
fearful of doctors or being found in Paris.

The last I saw of him was in the morgue
where he couldn't stop me visiting.

Squaring the Circle

These London squares: green thoughts in a grey mind,
like ample zoo enclosures that help keep
the animals sane. In Queen Square between
Faber and the Homeopathic Hospital
you did a weekly stint at, your colleagues planted
a memorial magnolia sapling
I thought too waxy-pale and ceremonial
but we turned up to its launch, or berthing,
grateful to them, and I've kept a bespoke,
black-and-white photo of it in full leaf
in sight of my desk. I never had you down
as a fully-fledged tree-hugger but then,
once, quite out-of-character, in earnest,
you argued and argued with a neighbour
blithely sawing down his copper beech
as if you'd heard a cry come from the gash.

Despite the blue, ribbed, plastic pipe dug in
to mainline water to its roots, the magnolia
only flourished a year, then ailed and died.
Now even the label with your name and dates
has gone, though the pipe remains, half-covered
with grass, a dark zero, a tiny circle in the square –
airhole, earhole, manhole, wormhole
to the underworld which still seems to listen out
for news of us as I pause and pass. I'd like
to plant another, sturdier tree there
but perhaps that gap in the grass is sign
enough. If laughs have accents, yours was always

unadorned Runcorn – I can hear it again
mocking this solemn stuff, full of round holes,
making clear it's not like either one of us
actually belongs in any London square.

Natural History

We never saw the blind, white salamander
in the Škocjan caves, nor the snow vole for that matter,
but out in the daylight on the karst plateau,
above the chasms and sinkholes, we came upon
a chapel in a forest of hornbeam and pine
whose mural shows a pious procession
mocked by a troupe of dwarfish louts.
With infectious fun, they caper and jeer
– one dances a jig, one squats and bares his bum
while a select crew from the animal kingdom
parade their own and nature's unconcern.
In their midst stands a big bird like a black swan
except its beak has declared independence
and become an enormous promontory.
I took this tufty, senile-looking creature
as a daft invention, the painter's *jeu d'esprit*,
but the verger said the bird was real enough
though killed off here four centuries ago.
Till now two small endangered colonies
have been holding out in Morocco
and a few breeding pairs have been spotted
in the Ethiopian highlands. Otherwise
that bird is history. And it's taken me
a year to hunt down its name in English:
the Northern Bald Ibis,
aka *geronticus eremita* –
its absence for so long witnessed and housed
in that old forest hermitage – it's the spitting
image of its portrait, with gelled, spiked plumes
for a nuchal ruff and a bare red face that's fastened

onto that barge-pole conk, an implement to feast
on lizards, scorpions and locusts.
Usually silent, it emits the odd hiss or else a grunt
for purposes of display or homecoming.

Azurite

It's azurite, he said, makes the pool blue.
A green-tinged blue Venetian artists used
for painting sea, keeping lapis lazuli
for their hazy, angel-haunted skies.
We'd driven out to the ramshackle farm,
where the farmer's son had filled a paddock
with scrapped cars as a commercial sideline,
to find your dented Audi a replacement door.

You'd have thought the pool might have given him
pause, with the pride he took in it, might have made
him wonder whether that seepage of oil,
those rusting wrecks were its best protection.
It was like Paul Nash's aircraft graveyard,
all lunar mashed metallic celery,
but that was wartime Cowley 1940,
this the gorse-flecked Ridgeway

a decade ago. So now I've forgotten
how to get there and if you ever got the door
though I remember the pool's oblivious blue,
how I scooped up a chill palmful
surprised it was colourless and how
speckled trout all facing an invisible altar
hung in the uplift, their eyes unlidded,
while the azure current coiled about them.

When I call on you, drained, bandaged, far removed
from any words, from the craft that
you've lifted up and left your mark on,
I lapse into silence and stare at
the tumbled lump of malachite that's been
lying on your garden table – its seams of green
are what azurite becomes when exposed
to air, black-banded but still bright as life.

King Billy's Nemesis

Mouldywarp, thrower of dirt,
has tripped the horse called Sorrel
and broke the royal collarbone and killed
the King of England.

Though Jacobites toasted the little gentleman
in the black velvet waistcoat,
if push came to shove he was always
more of a Republican

and apart from a walk-on role
as the ghost of King Hamlet
till then he'd rarely shown
much passion for politics.

Three hundred years he's laid low,
airing the earth and stocking his larder
with shelf-fulls of worms,
live worms as it happens.

But today he broached the deep snow
and left one flaw in the perfect
field of white – black earth
at its core and an oval

aureole of cindery grey
with an equal mix of snow and soil.
Looks like a black wig
riding a white steed.

Now he's backed up down into the dark,
same old mole, with a bow and a scrape
or was that a wave
from his shovel-shaped mitt?

'He "Digesteth Harde Yron"'

Or rather the ostrich, like the crocodile,
swallows hard stones such as quartz or granite
which jostle in the gizzard to assist
the slow work of digestion.

Such was the work required to mill
a wide diet of New Zealand vegetation
that the enormous moas
went miles in search of the right stones

which can be found beside their skeletons
or when the bones have long been broken down
as phantom tracts, as cairns to their extinction,
all immaculately polished and rounded.

The Fly Inventory

The fly by night.
The fly in the ointment.
The fly in amber.
The fly on the wall.
The fly on the wall
in Hans Memling's *Portrait of a Carthusian*
often considered a *memento mori*
though it could be a demonic distraction from prayer.
Or a model of seraphic stillness.
Holub's fly at the Battle of Crécy.
The five kinds of fly I counted today
on a single umbel of the yarrow
including a greenbottle,
with crimson headlights and cupreous bodywork,
avidly hoovering pollen
through a black trumpet thicker than its legs.
The black-and-white human fly by Luc Tuymans
undergoing a sinister metamorphosis.
The fly in the film *The Fly*.
The fly in the remake *The Fly*.
The fly on the frieze in the *mercato di lana* at Pompeii.
The fly that bit the flying horse that caused the fall
of Bellerephon into a thorn bush.
The fly without teeth
but a copious supply of saliva.
The fly in the coal-shed that Mahon
set beside the *Winged Victory of Samothrace*,
so braced against each other it's hard to know
which of them he thought up first.
The flies of Machado, Blake and Dickinson.

But that's enough fly poems
though there's also 'the marble fly': Mandelstam's nickname.
The fly's stealthy ovipositor
that prises open a dead linnet's beak
under the patient eye of Jean Henri Fabre.
Una mosca muerta: used of someone not especially attractive.
The fly on the pedestal not yet constructed
in the *plaza major* of the city of flies.
Beelzebub, the lord of the flies.
The fly within, the inner fly.
The fly that flew from the list of flies.
The fly that stops its din when you switch the light off
but starts again at dawn, and needs to check
whether you're still among the quick or dead.
The fly whisk; the fly swatter; fly spray;
The Fully Guaranteed Electric Fly Killer
– escalations in the war against the fly.
The fly that survived.

The Possessors

The only things that animals possess,
apart from parasites, are what they hold
between their teeth. But that they won't release.
Though even this doubtful knowledge is possession,
the snap and grip of our champion mammal
the hyena exerts a 1,000 lbs of pressure.

Whereas the least adept of us will carry
a shopping bag stuffed with old newspapers
or wheel a rusty trolley through the streets
with a cargo of obscure prestige.
And see what happens when you try to steal it.

The less we have, the more it seems we've failed
to make our way. I miss that less, and used to travel
light but now I'm like an overburdened camel
wedged in the strait gate of Jerusalem.

Guilt

Last night asleep I killed a poet
and nothing I did could resurrect him.
The shopping mall's defibrillator kit

was useless, and I drew the line at mouth-to-mouth.
Awake, the guilt remained – although he wasn't
even a good poet. Well, to be fair, there are worse.

I'd never had the least intent to harm him
unless an involuntary expression of disdain
and the absence of a single word of praise

makes one a murderer. It's not as though
his talents have gone unsung – sung, they've been,
by a choir of critics. If I were to say

what irks me especially in his work,
he could put a name, his own name, to this:
he'd know it was him that I'd killed, and me

that had killed him, and then I'd have only
added insult to mortal injury.
It should ease my mind that there's no body,

no cordoned crime site, no chalk outline,
no weapon, no discernible motive.
But there it is: his blood is on my hands.

Micropoems

Leonardo Sinisgalli, from Mosche in bottiglie

Bad Friend (1)

The bad friend
has some good news
to hide from you.

Bad Friend (2)

In sight of treasure
he tells you to turn.

Black Book

Another name
in the book of
lost friends.

Shadow

The shadow of a rectangle
is always a rectangle;
though the shadow of a circle's
almost never a circle.

The Mothers

Far from being goddesses or sibyls:
the poor mothers
suffering from migraine
crushed by the heart's servitude.

I Estranged Myself

I estranged myself
not wanting either
accomplices or companions.

Dear Life

Dear life,
you chose colourless places,
anonymous hours,
the tritest occasions.
You chose the wrong companions.

Ouch

It takes genius to make a language,
to draw nails out with your teeth.

Stricken Proverbs

A full vessel is inaudible.

*

Every cliff has a glass edge,
every chasm a covering cloud.
Every lining has a hidden needle.

*

Many a sickle rakes the stubble.

*

A rip in space needs a stitch in time.

*

Time's flies wait to feast on no man.

*

Art longs for the brevity of life.

*

Never a nail in the blacksmith's forge,
nor a pen in the poet's pocket.

*

Home is where the heart can't live.

*

All Rome leads to are roads.

*

For the deep well: a long cord and a light bucket.

*

Where there's a will, there's a wall.

Entropy in Wiesbaden

David Huerta, 'Entropia en Wiesbaden'

You peeped out over the Roman wall
into the German street
battered by the slant, stubborn rain.
What you saw was Europe worn away,
its crowded, fractal script.
Lots of money, well-cut clothes,
prim dwellings, curt gestures,
ghastly food – and, finally, Goethe
in his memorious, courtier mode,
patriarch, *santo doctus*, mode
of the all-enlightened poet.
Nothing to tell on your return
except for the now constant,
final rain. A breath of the Holy Spirit
entered the mouth of the passing moment –
but you, present, more diligent
with detail than the Middle Ages
of the Black Forest,
bore witness to the puritan sermon
and the post-industrial dust,
the overbearing views of
some academic, the counsel
of an editor astray
in Frankfurt. Entropy
engulfed Wiesbaden
while over and over you were reborn
against the blaze of time.

Outcast

I savour the notes of the symphony
the way an ugly troll gawps at Aphrodite,
as at an order way beyond all comprehension

that would lift me up to its hallowed height
if I weren't so incurably deaf and squat.
Suffer the tuneless to come unto thee,

god of the hollow lute and the flute,
though we have no emptiness to resonate
being chockful of splintery dissonance.

The first shall be first, and the last, last –
left outside the concert to imagine
seraphic bow-sweeps and the baton's dance.

One Day

I shall pick up and play the violin
my hopeful great-uncle made for me
out of seventy-odd planished bits of maple,

its scrolled head a ruby-tinted fern.
It sailed across the ocean in a coffin
and is still stretched out in a velvet box,

the E string snapped like a sawn cable.
A musician who played it judged it a fine
big-voiced burly fiddle

though with a wolf note in the upper reaches.
Wolf note to which I'm perfectly attuned.